The Codependency Help Book

How to Fix a Codependent Relationship

Rob Watts

Copyright © 2019 Rob Watts

All rights reserved.

ISBN-13: 978-1-0762-3261-8

© COPYRIGHT 2019 BY **ROB WATTS** - ALL RIGHTS RESERVED.

The content contained within this book may not be reproduced, duplicated or transmitted without direct written permission from the author or the publisher.

Under no circumstances will any blame or legal responsibility be held against the publisher, or author, for any damages, reparation, or monetary loss due to the information contained within this book. Either directly or indirectly.

Legal Notice:
This book is copyright protected. This book is only for personal use. You cannot amend, distribute, sell, use, quote or paraphrase any part, or the content within this book, without the consent of the author or publisher.

Disclaimer Notice:
Please note the information contained within this document is for educational and entertainment purposes only. All effort has been executed to present accurate, up to date, and reliable, complete information. No warranties of any kind are declared or implied. Readers acknowledge that the author is not engaging in the rendering of legal, financial, medical or professional advice. The content within this book has been derived from various sources. Please consult a licensed professional before attempting any techniques outlined in this book.

By reading this book, the reader agrees that under no circumstances is the author responsible for any losses, direct or indirect, which are incurred as a result of the use of information contained within this document, including, but not limited to, — errors, omissions, or inaccuracies..

CONTENTS

	Introduction	1
1	Getting Acquainted with the Concept of Codependency	3
2	Detailing Codependent vs. Interdependent Relationship	12
3	Factors That Create Codependency	18
4	Factors That Sustain Codependency: The Snowball Effect	26
5	Ways to Recover from a Codependent Relationship	32
	Conclusion	38

INTRODUCTION

Most people believe relationships are blissful only during the initial stage, but that's not true. There are older couples who value and appreciate their relationships, so the concept of "it only tastes good in the beginning" is not true. It is in the hands of the individuals to shape their relationships meaningfully. It is essential to have self-respect and self-esteem to maintain a healthy relationship. If you don't value your own self, how will you think about another individual's respect and self-worth?

The main reason why codependent relationships are common is that people fail to value their own self. But that's just one of the reasons, which means you will find more reasons that trigger a codependent relationship in this book. As an individual, you must make sure to take necessary actions once you find yourself in an unhealthy relationship.

To fix or to move out from a codependent relationship, you must make sure to understand what 'codependency' means. Only after understanding the term 'codependency' and the reasons why it is being created, will you be able to find a solution for it. You shouldn't let unhealthy relationships remain that way because it will end up creating a lot of problems to your self-esteem and overall well-being. Yes, your relationship has a lot to do with your well-being. If your mental health is not in a positive state, it may affect your overall health.

Through this guide, you will find how people become dependent on another individual and why they find it hard to move out or fix a codependent relationship. You will find the reasons that sustain codependency. However, that's not all; this guide will provide tips to recover from codependent relationships and to lead a happy life.

Of course, it is not going to be easy to become an independent individual. It will not be easy to move away or keep a distance from the person whom you were codependent on, but with time, you will taste the beauty of being yourself. You will value your presence and how important it is to give time for yourself. When you give time for yourself, you will discover more opportunities and paths to grow. Hence, it is crucial to fix or to overcome a codependent relationship before it is too late. Using this self-help guide, you can build a better version of yourself without letting yourself fall into the trap of codependency!

Happy reading!

1 GETTING ACQUAINTED WITH THE CONCEPT OF CODEPENDENCY

People often confuse 'love' and 'codependency,' and they assume once you are in a relationship, you must not put your own needs forward. You have to sacrifice a lot of things to keep your partner happy, but do you get the favor in return? Of course, you can do anything out of 'love,' but once it becomes a factor that holds you captivated, then, it is no longer 'love' but it is 'codependency.' You must understand the difference between love and codependency if you want to remain in a healthy relationship.

Different people might provide different definition for codependency by analyzing their own situation. But ultimately, it is about giving your level best to your relationship while your partner doesn't even care to do so. In most relationships, one partner needs more attention than the other; when this happens, the rate of dependency increases. For example, if you think about a relationship with a narcissist, you will find yourself as a giver. No matter how much you give, your partner will want more until you are worn out. Just like being involved with a narcissist, you'll be the one to be blamed and tortured when you are in a codependent relationship.

When an individual in a healthy relationship requires support and comfort, it is normal. You will need your partner's support and comfort in critical situations, but if you are seeking validation from your partner for being yourself, then it is different than a healthy relationship. A relationship should have a balance. Without balance, it becomes messy. Hence, the mutual connection between you and your partner should be genuine, not forceful. However, it is essential to understand the concept of codependency if you want to know whether you are in an unhealthy relationship.

Codependency is a passed down behavior that keeps coming from every generation. This behavior does not let an individual enjoy a healthy relationship because of the emotional condition. Often codependency deals with relationships that are abusive because those relationships are like a one-way transaction. One of the individuals gets all the benefits and happiness from the relationship, whereas the other partner gets nothing. There are different reasons why codependency gets carried forward, and I'll cover them in the following chapters.

Actually, it is easy to understand when you are in a codependent relationship because it will be clear when you seek validation from your partner for your identity. You are in a codependent relationship the moment your goals and aims are centered around your partner even though ultimate sacrifices are made. You'll slowly lose the autonomy even before you know it and it is not healthy.

Codependency can affect anybody. Not only romantic relationships but also any other relationship can be affected by codependency. Initially, the term codependency was related to chemical dependency, but now, it has broadened towards people-relationships as well. When an individual is in a relationship with a mentally ill person or someone from a dysfunctional family, the relationship often turns out codependent. If you are wondering how a person from a dysfunctional family can create a codependent relationship, keep reading. The dysfunctional family deals with members that suffer from pain, anger, hatred, fear, and denial. There are several underlying reasons, such as addiction, sexual abuse, and chronic mental illness.

Unfortunately, dysfunctional families aren't ready to acknowledge the problem. They don't spend time to discuss or confront the issue. They tend to conceal the problem, which leads to further issues. The members of dysfunctional families learn to avoid their own needs and become the ones who "survive" instead of the ones who "live." Denying and ignoring complex emotions will not help them to lead a happy life, but that's how members from dysfunctional families live. The complete attention and focus will be on the addicted family member. The codependent family member will be spending his or her life taking care of the sick while sacrificing their own needs. Of course, you must take care of a sick person, but shouldn't you be concerned about your own health too? That balance doesn't happen in a dysfunctional family. This is how members from dysfunctional families give life to codependent relationships. But do you know how codependent individuals behave?

The most common trait one can see in a codependent person is their low self-esteem. They tend to search for everything outside of themselves, even though they are capable of finding it within themselves. They feel insecure in their own skin and personality, which is disheartening. It is beautiful that they want to take care of the other individual, but in the process of taking care of the other individual, they lose themselves.

When you become dependent on another individual, it becomes difficult to move out of the cycle. Also, don't ever think a 'breakup' will clear up the path for you because it will not. You might get back with the same person once again because you have gotten used to being dependent on him or her. One of my friends has been in a similar situation. She's intelligent and capable of doing anything. But she was in a codependent relationship and had to ask permission for every single thing, had to put forward his needs over hers. This was a huge barrier in reaching her goals. Of course, he was obsessed with her and wasn't ready for a breakup. Even after breaking up, he kept coming back, and she accepted him over and over again. But finally, she understood the negative impact caused by codependency, and she moved away from him gradually while improving her own self. Luckily, she's pursuing all her dreams and goals. Even though I easily said it in a few lines, it wasn't easy for her to move out. She fought her own self!

You see, a codependent relationship is a real threat so you must sort it as soon as possible. There are a few characteristics of codependents that you must be aware of:
- They feel responsible for other's actions.
- They confuse the meaning of pity and love.
- They feel obliged to do more than they should.
- They tend to get hurt if their efforts aren't recognized.
- They are ready to do anything to hold on to the relationship.
- They have a real need for recognition.
- They are interested in approval.
- They have a great interest in controlling others.
- They don't trust themselves or others.
- They don't like being alone or abandoned.
- They are not ready to adjust.
- They have problems with intimacy.
- They have chronic anger.
- They are dishonest.
- They struggle to make decisions, but they make decisions for others.

It is vital to treat codependency because it is rooted in the person since childhood. Even if you read self-help guides and blogs, it is essential to get professional help. The treatment will be done by analyzing childhood issues and current behaviors. Most treatments include experiential groups, education, and support to rediscover one's self. A professional will dig the issues from the root so that it can be treated from scratch. Codependents are created at home, so the change should begin at home. Dysfunctional families should be taught and guided regarding codependency and how to fix it. There are health centers, abuse treatment centers, and many more programs that will help you to fix or overcome codependency. Psychotherapy is one of the recommended treatments because codependency is related to personality issues. It is tough to overcome codependency all alone, so the support of a therapist is required and beneficial. But when you are finding a therapist, it is essential to find the right therapist.

How Codependency Works

Once you understand the term 'codependency,' you must think about the way codependency works in a relationship. How does a codependent relationship work? How would you know if you are in a codependent relationship? Some codependent relationships are unbreakable due to certain reasons. Most people tend to get back with the same person even though the relationship is unhealthy. You may have encountered couples who aren't happy with their relationship, yet they tend to stick together. I have encountered so many couples who blame their partner, yet remain with the same person. One thing I have noticed in all the couples who stick together even though they don't have a healthy relationship is they don't grow as individual people. They remain where they were when they started the relationship. This is not something to be happy about because a healthy relationship will help you to grow as a person.

They remain in unhealthy relationships due to different reasons such as children, shame, finances, and the time invested in the relationship. For example, they fear that other people might blame or shame them for ending the relationship, which is why they try to hold on to the relationship even if they aren't happy. But don't you think it is important to worry about your own happiness than to think about other people's opinion about your relationship? If you find that you are in a codependent relationship, you must not think about others' opinions or any other reasons, instead, think about yourself and happiness.

However, it is also essential to understand the underlying reasons why a person may be codependent, so let me make it clear for you. We are vulnerable at birth, and we are totally dependent on safety, regulation, and food provided by the caregivers. It is crucial for the infant to be attached to the caregiver because it fulfills the emotional needs of the infant. But in the absence of a caregiver, the child doesn't play the role of a dependent. Hence, dysfunctional families create such characters and avoid the problem altogether. When such children grow up, they tend to hold their behaviors even when they engage in adult relationships.

Obviously, dissatisfaction builds when you don't understand your wants and needs just because you are obsessed with being the "boss" in your relationship. You tend to overreact when the partner doesn't listen or lets you down. You don't have the self-control and the internal focus, hence, you try to control your partner and seek validation so that you are pleased. You like to be bossy while making unreasonable commands and expect your partner to obey your commands. When you understand that you are unable to control your partner, you become disappointed and might even reach depression. This will not help your relationship nor your life.

You have to focus on being a self-reliant individual who is capable of nurturing your own needs. You should get connected to your own world if you want to overcome codependency. It takes a lot of courage to wave goodbye to unhealthy behaviors, yet it is worth it. If you don't stop your caretaking behaviors, you will not be able to remain in a healthy relationship. You must learn to respond, not react because when you react, you become bossy and try to control others, including your partner. This will kill your own happiness and peace. You must build yourself once again to accept 'no' as an answer from your partner and others. The moment you overcome codependency, you will find the genuine happiness that you were missing all this time. You will feel comfortable when you walk away from a relationship. However, there are different facets related to codependency, which you must know about.

Did you know codependency has enduring symptoms that can increase over time if not treated properly? If you don't get proper treatments, you might have to struggle in the long run. Although we've discussed that the dysfunctional family is one of the significant reasons for codependency, it is essential to understand the concept in-depth. Of course, it might be the family environment that creates codependents, but it is not possible to identify dependency in the early stages of family life, because children are dependent. Only after they reach adulthood, it is possible to diagnose codependency. Moreover, codependency will be identifiable when close relationships are formed. So when you get involved in intimate relationships, it is easy to witness codependency in different facets.

Facet One

The facet one of close relationship will be about romance. You might offer extra attention and interest for your partner, and you might be overly prepared for him or her. But when you deal with codependency, romance and the relationship reaches a level of obsession. You will find all of his or her behaviors problematic. Doubt and suspicion will increase, and also you'll give up your friends and your own needs for him or her.

Facet Two

When you reach the second facet of your relationship, you will insert more effort to reduce the painful situations that occurred in the relationship, but then, self-blame is created. With time, you will realize that your level of self-esteem reduces. And you will end up compromising a lot of yourself to protect your relationship. But don't think sacrificing your own happiness will lead towards anything useful; rather your anger and resentment will increase. At the same time, you will manipulate, blame, or nag your partner because you need him or her to change.

Facet Three

In the third facet, things turn out worse because this is when you develop emotional and physical symptoms that affect your health. You may encounter sleep problems, digestive issues, stress-related disorder, eating disorders, heart disease, allergies, and headaches. In the meantime, other addictions will increase while you lack self-care and self-esteem.

You'd have gone through all these facets when you understand that you are codependent. Yes, it might feel okay to give your best for a relationship. You might be ready to invest all your time in the relationship just to shape it up perfectly. Reaching an extra mile to keep your partner happy, loved, and secure will not be a big deal for you. It's absolutely alright to treat your partner in the best possible way, but too much of anything is good for nothing. You must have a clear vision about a healthy and codependent relationship because the outcome of a codependent relationship is enormous.

Usually, a codependent relationship is intense. Even if thousands of problems come up, the codependent partner will somehow try to stick with their partner. Also, the codependent partner will be ready to give all the time and effort to keep the relationship going. More often, you tend to see your relationship as the ONLY valuable thing in the whole universe. As I mentioned in the beginning, you should not confuse 'love,' and 'codependency' so here are a few ways indicators of a codependent relationship:

You Feel That the Relationship is Unbalanced

Most healthy relationships lose the perfect balance but that doesn't mean that those relationships have no balance. However, when you think about a codependent relationship, it is unbalanced. It becomes one-sided where only one partner does and provides everything, whereas the other doesn't even bother. Unlike healthy relationships, you will not witness support and love even during hard times because it is not how codependent relationship work. Most of the time, if your relationship is all about one person giving, it means you are in a codependent relationship. Reciprocated sacrifices shape up a good relationship. Think about how you behave and handle things within a relationship so that the reality will settle in.

You Start to Feel and Consider Your Partner's Pain as Yours

Nobody likes to see their loved ones hurt or sick. You may help your partner to recover when he or she is sick, and this is not something terrible. Of course, you must help another individual when they struggle. But the problem is when you exceed your limit and consider your partner's pain like yours. When this happens, you should know that it is codependency. If you don't think about your own health and well-being just because you want to take care of your partner, then it is a severe problem that needs treatment.

You Try to be Very "Understanding."

First of all, you must understand what it means to be an understanding partner. If you understand your partner's anger, it is a good sign. But letting your partner scold you without a valid reason is not understanding. If your partner loses his or her patience once or twice, it is okay. But if it happens repeatedly and if you are ignoring it in the name of understanding, it is not so-called understanding! It is CODEPENDENCY and let that sink in. Accepting your partner's anger even though it is not reasonable is not a sign for a healthy relationship. Partners should take responsibility for what they do and speak!

You are Ready to do Anything for Your Partner

Most common factors of codependency are the fear of losing your partner. This fear grows jealousy and obsessions, and so it becomes difficult for the other person to remain with you. In a healthy relationship, one partner will expect another partner to reciprocate his or her feelings so that there is a mutual connection. But a codependent person will not worry about reciprocating feelings. Instead, you will do all the possible things to save your relationship. Your only focus would be to satisfy the needs of your partner. Even if you encounter justifiable behaviors, you will still ignore or tolerate them because you believe it is worthy! For example, even if you find your partner is cheating, you will just ignore it because he or she is with you despite the cheating.

You Value the Term "We."

When you become obsessed with your relationship, you tend to do things together, and you don't like doing anything alone. You make an effort to relate to your partner as much as possible. The way you rely on your partner will keep increasing; for example, you will look for emotional support, affection, and even self-worth. On the other hand, healthy relationships nurture both individuals. They have space, and they make an effort to grow on their own path. They are independent individuals who can do the things they wish on their own. Of course, it is good to consider the term "we," but not by concealing the term "I."

You Are Obliged to Become the Rescuer

You can't become the rescuer of your partner each time he or she falls into trouble. But most codependent people are obliged to become the rescuer. They think by rescuing they will be able to attract and captivate the partner. But it doesn't work that way, and this clearly indicates the sign of a codependent relationship.

You Accept Them Along with Their Toxic Flaws

Yes, you have to love someone for who they are. But if you love your partner along with his or her toxic flaws, it doesn't justify the statement. As a codependent, you manipulate your expectations about your partner and set unrealistic demands. In a healthy relationship, individuals accept one another for who they are, but they make sure to correct the toxic flaws if they come across any because it is essential.

Once you realize that you are in a codependent relationship, you must do the essentials to fix it. You must pause and think about your behaviors and find ways to correct them. You must think about what you really want from the relationship. I know it is not going to be easy. It's also important to realize that being codependent doesn't make you arrogant, because you may truly love him or her. The problem is you don't treat your relationship like the normal ones, and rather you look for emotional fulfillment that you can't get from anywhere else.

Before you move on with the codependent relationship, you must ask yourself whether you really need this or it is high time to discover yourself first! There are a lot more details to be discussed, so continue reading.

2 DETAILING CODEPENDENT VS. INTERDEPENDENT RELATIONSHIP

Codependent Relationship

You know codependency is a learned behavior. It would have been around since long ago, but people couldn't identify or realize it. However, codependency kills an individual's true nature by making him or her suffer all alone. Codependency can be treated if identified. Actually, there are different definitions for codependency, but when you narrow them down, you will end up with a single definition; an addictive unhealthy relationship with dysfunctional boundaries. First, codependency was all about the ones who lived and addressed the needs of drug abusers and alcoholics. But over time, the definition of codependency expanded to include unhealthy relationships that don't allow the other person to grow. If you are someone who has adopted a great deal of pain so that you could survive, then you belong to the category of codependents. To be said simply, codependency is a byproduct of the traumatic stress response.

That said, it is essential to understand how codependent relationships work. Basically, those relationships don't have the balance it should because both people are overly dependent on one another. When both the partners rely on one another while exceeding the reasonable limit, it puts the relationship off balance. When the partners somehow try to make up and keep going, it affects their lives severely. Both partners lose their real identities. They struggle to develop personally and professionally because codependency rules their relationship. They don't reciprocate sacrifices, emotions, and feelings. They don't confront doubts and fears, and it is not at all healthy because how can you live by denying the obvious things?

Unlike the interdependent relationship, codependents want to feel the presence of their partner to become okay.

They always look for validation from their partner, and the partner gets used to this method, so he or she feels superior. For example, seeking permission to hang out with your own friends becomes a habit, and in case, you don't seek permission your partner might create a scene. Actually, your partner is not at fault in this case because you have created the habit and even when he or she scolds for not seeking permission, you start saying "sorry" and match it up without discussing the actual problem. You fear that you might lose your partner if you don't patch up and you believe your partner is right about everything. This is not a healthy relationship because a healthy relationship is about equality and understanding!

Even if the codependent person feels unworthy, insecure, and lonely, he or she will still do anything to keep the partner happy and content. Also, codependent relationships are greedy for power and control. Sometimes, one partner might have all the power to control the other, or the other partner would have the complete responsibility for their partner. Somehow, it doesn't qualify as an inmate relationship because it looks more like unhealthy parenting. The codependents will not be happy in a relationship because common feelings of a codependent are resentfulness, guilt, and anxiety. The codependents assume that they are responsible for their partner's happiness and sadness. To make this happen, the partners reach out to each other to make themselves okay. They don't respect one another for who they are because they always want to correct their partners. The relationship will feel like a cage because it doesn't let the individual grow.

In a codependent relationship, both the partners may look healthy and happy, but they are actually not happy and healthy. Both adults feel insecure and overly dependent on one another. The problem is when one partner relies on the emotional stability of the other. The codependents look as if they are independent, but they are not. They portray themselves as needy so that they get the attention and validation required. However, relationships like this will create pressure, anxiety, anger, and depression You must be happy and relaxed when you are in a relationship. Moreover, the relationship should help you grow without clipping your wings.

Some of the traits you can notice in a codependent relationship:
- Poor to no boundaries
- Unhealthy communication
- People pleasing nature
- Manipulation and reactivity

- Hardships with emotional intimacy
- Blaming and controlling one another
- Low self-esteem
- Trust issues
- No place for personal growth
- Not interested in anything apart from the relationship

So when you are in a codependent relationship, you can't expect autonomy. You will not have room for growth. In a codependent relationship, often both partners feel guilty because of their inability to handle the relationship successfully. Do you want to remain in a relationship that ruins you and your partner's life?

Interdependent Relationship

So far, you have learned about codependency in detail, now let me explain independent relationship because it is essential to what a healthy relationship looks like. We all value relationships because of the colors it adds to our lives. Through healthy bonds, relationships are taken to a better level. If you look at a healthy long-term relationship, you can clearly see that the bond is based on emotional connection. As a codependent person, even you might be wanting a healthy relationship because it keeps you happy and healthy. But how can you build such a relationship? And how do other people build an interdependent relationship? Don't you dream of a relationship that has your back and supports your growth? It is possible to build that kind of relationship if both partners understand the meaning of a healthy relationship.

Before we dig deeper, let's understand interdependency. An interdependent relationship is when the partners understand the value of emotions and respect each other's emotions while building a steady relationship. Both the partners make an effort to understand emotional intimacy in a relationship. Also, in an interdependent relationship, both of the partners will let each other reach their goals and aims in life.

If you think about the concept of codependency, it might depress you because it is not healthy. You'll be needing someone by your side to validate your presence. But when you are in an interdependent relationship, you will understand that independence matters a lot more than dependence. You must enjoy your freedom without having to sacrifice the bond created between you and your partner. When you reach an extreme level of independence, you will end up devaluing your partner's presence. Hence, everything in life should be at a moderate level.

You must understand the clear difference between interdependence and codependency. A codependent couple will not make an effort to think about their own self, whereas an interdependent couple will respect their own self. Codependents believe that they should meet their partners' needs perfectly, even if their own needs are sacrificed. Also, they always want to be wanted so that it gives the sense of being present or alive.

If you are in an interdependent relationship, you can enjoy the following:
- You have the freedom of choice, so personal growth is highly promoted.
- You receive your partner's support to grow and develop in your own way.
- Your views and opinions will be respected.
- You have high self-esteem, values, and individual identities. Also, your self-esteem will not be influenced by your partner because that is not what self-esteem is all about.
- You and your partner will be working toward a mutual goal.
- You have your partner's help whenever you are in a critical situation.
- You engage in different activities so that it builds a balance in your relationship. When you focus only on the relationship, you tend to lose the balance.
- You care and sympathize with your partner, but that doesn't make you want to end his or her problems while forgetting yours. Instead, you let your partner handle it alone so that he or she becomes stronger and capable.
- You are ready for healthy changes when required.
- You have a mutual understanding.
- You have integrity and honesty in your relationship. If there are any issues, you and your partner discuss and sort them out.
- You build a relationship on trust, love, and understanding.

So now you know why an interdependent relationship is healthy. When your relationship has the balance it should have, you will be able to focus on all the other things in life. You and your partner can focus on healthy ways to meet each other's needs, both mentally and physically. You will not feel suffocated by the other person. You don't have to ignore your own needs for him or her. When you let your partner make his or her decision, you will have time for your life and decisions. There will be room for self-improvement so you can grow better. Also, when you don't have to worry about your relationship, you'll have the peace of mind that is needed to lead a happy life!

You can easily identify a healthy relationship if the relationship has the following traits:
- Proper communication
- Listening and expressing
- Healthy boundaries
- Room for personal growth and interest
- Taking responsibility for their mistakes
- Responding to each other in a decent manner
- Respecting each other
- Healthy self-esteem
- Being approachable and honest

You might have heard people say that their relationships are like "safe haven," and they would have meant interdependent relationships. If you are an in an interdependent relationship, you'd feel the same. When you are in an interdependent relationship, you will feel that you can trust and turn towards your partner because the bond is strong and healthy!

So, do you think you can create an interdependent relationship? Of course, you can. You just need to learn the ways to create an interdependent relationship. First of all, you must know that being mindful of who you are is essential to build a relationship with another individual. Mostly, people enter into relationships because they want to feel a sense of belonging and to avoid loneliness. Well, these reasons aren't the reasons why you should enter into a relationship. Before you begin a relationship with another individual, you must make sure to do self-reflection. You must have the values that you respect. You must know why you want to enter into a relationship, or you want to be with that person. It is essential to know yourself before you make an effort to understand another individual.

Moreover, you should not lose yourself once you get into a relationship. You must know the following tips in mind:
- You must know what you desire and what's essential for you
- You must not step back when you want to say or ask something
- You must not negotiate the time that you spend with family and friends
- You must not give up your goals and aims.
- You don't have to overlook your values.
- You should find time for interests and hobbies.
- You don't have to say "yes" always
- You shouldn't become a people-pleaser

If you follow all these tips, you will become a better version of yourself. But to establish an interdependent relationship, your partner should follow the same tips as well. Actually, both you and your partner should focus on yourselves and personal growth. When both of you are focused on personal growth and development, it is easy to lead a healthy relationship. When you follow this method, you wouldn't have to worry about losing your partner because you've built self-worth. When your relationship is interdependent, you will not feel guilty or scared because it is established safely. To lead a happy and healthy relationship, you must reflect on yourself not only when you start a relationship, but also throughout the relationship. You must encourage your partner as well, so it becomes a mutual goal.

3 FACTORS THAT CREATE CODEPENDENCY

Once you get an explicit knowledge of the concept of codependency, you must find the factors that create codependency. From where does it start? Why does it affect your relationship? How can you break the habit of controlling someone? Initially, you might wonder whether it is wrong to be kind to others, but it is not the case. Different factors create codependency, but for most people, codependency starts from childhood. It is impossible to correct codependency when you are a child because you are not aware of it. When you were a child, you did not have enough experience or cognitive abilities to understand unhealthy relationships.

Normally, if both parents are addicts or suffer from illness, it is obvious that the home doesn't represent a typical home. In such a situation, the children become the victim, and they sacrifice their childhood to meet the responsibilities of the parents. They make sure that their siblings are fed and other important responsibilities are fulfilled. When a child plays the role of a parent, the true self of the child gets lost. The children who come from a dysfunctional family will ensure to keep everyone happy even if their own happiness is taken for grant. They are the ones who give without expecting anything in return. They will not speak up to solve their issues or discuss their pain. They will rely on others' satisfaction to meet their emotional fulfillment. If you can relate to this, it means you have to overcome codependency to lead a happy life. Now is the time to focus on yourself even if it did not matter before. However, let's see all the major factors that create codependency so that you can remove it from the root.

Aggrieved Desires

The relationship between codependency and childhood is clear; now let's learn the connection between aggrieved desires and codependency. As much as childhood is considered a factor that creates codependency, aggrieved desires are also one of the factors. If you tend to focus on others' needs above yours, then you are likely to experience aggrieved desires. When you do things at your own expenses, there are so many negative feelings that build up in your mind. Over time, these negative feelings will give life to resentment or aggrieved desires. But you must understand that your codependent behaviors will harm not only you, but also the other person.

Sometimes, people refer to codependency as relationship addiction. If you think about other addictions such as drugs and alcohol, it is possible to recover through direct methods. But relationship addiction is not as straightforward as other addictions. Even if you want to recover from relationship addiction, you can't do it directly. How can you stop caring and loving someone? You can't easily, so steps to recovery should be smooth and steady.

Of course, helping others is good, but only when you exceed the limit do the problems get created, and the value of helping reduces. In a codependent relationship, one partner will lose their identity while making the other miserable. Another problem in a codependent relationship is the other partner get used to having someone by their side all the time. But the codependent individual does not get that support often, and somehow it creates aggrieved desires in the heart of the codependent. Because of the codependent partner, the recipient of the relationship tends to pass the ball to the codependent all the time without making an effort to solve the problems. They lose the motivation to improve their life because they have someone to uplift their life even if they don't.

On the upside, the codependents have a huge heart that accommodates everyone. They are ready to do anything for their relationship because they are incredibly loyal. Almost everything that they do, goes the extra mile. When you think about a healthy relationship, it doesn't center upon one person, and is mutual instead. Both the partners have their share of listening, talking, helping, and more.

When you belittle your needs in a relationship, you will end up creating an unhealthy relationship. The unhealthy relationship will trigger a lot of negative emotions and feelings even if you don't share them with your partner. So as an individual, you shouldn't bottle up emotions because, at a point, it might explode and create a huge mess. Similarly, your aggrieved desires will find its way out, but it will not end up positive. To treat aggrieved desires, you must overcome codependency.

However, overcoming codependency requires a lot of work because it is directly related to yourself. Self-analyzing is essential to understanding your level of codependency. When you are analyzing, you shouldn't take decisions on impulse because they are likely to go wrong. Your inner wisdom should be understood to make the right decision. If you can't handle yourself all alone, you must consult a therapist to help you out of this.

In all seriousness, it is not easy to be a codependent because it takes a lot of effort plus sacrifices to be one. Also, you should know that it is not worth it to become codependent as you or your partner don't benefit from it. You might come across a lot of emotional problems during this stage.

If you want to understand the codependent relationship, consider this example (characters are hypothetical). John and Lisa are a couple. But Lisa is codependent, so whenever John asks a favor, she doesn't turn it down. So one day, he wanted her to drive him to the airport because his car hasn't been repaired yet. Even though Lisa has laundry to do and a significant project to complete, she still says "okay," because she is not comfortable saying "no". Lisa is worried about John's accident even though drunken driving is a huge mistake. She is so concerned about his situation that she piled up laundry and work. Lisa, being codependent, wants to help John and make things easy for him. So even if driving to the airport will cost her a lot, she still makes up her mind to do it. The same codependent behavior tends to continue and cause a lot of problems in Lisa's life, although John has no idea about it.

We all get the support from our inner voice, and sometimes we listen but sometimes we don't. Codependents often avoid the inner voice and focus on doing what they usually do, just like the above example. If you elaborate on the above example, you will understand that Lisa's emotions during the car ride would have been complicated. Her codependent self would support her decision, whereas her inner voice creates resentment. This would have been hard for her. And if you have been in such a situation, you might understand her feelings better than anybody else.

Instead of saying "yes," Lisa could have said "no" in a polite manner. If Lisa and John were in a healthy relationship, he would have understood her and not asked for a ride in the first place. But you must understand that helping each other doesn't make your relationship unhealthy. Instead, it is the codependent way of helping your partner that kills the health of your relationship.

If you want to avoid aggrieved desires, you must make sure to stay in tune with your inner voice. It will help you make the right decision. You must look at the pros and cons before you provide an answer. You must think about your day-to-day activities before lending a helping hand. It is okay to sacrifice a few things to help another person, but don't make it a habit and trigger aggrieved desires. Here are some tips that you can use:

- Spend time for yourself and think about the ways to pamper yourself.
- You don't have to force yourself to say "yes" because it is not the ONLY option you have.
- Learn to say "no" even if it's hard.
- You don't have to take responsibility for someone else's life.
- Don't answer right away; take time and think about the answer you are going to provide.
- If you are not afraid, how would you react? Think about it.
- Prioritize your needs.
- Don't hold back your opinions and interest because even small things count. If you want to go to the movies, just say it. Or if you don't like a particular restaurant, be brave enough to say it. If you start small, you will be able to provide opinions and interest in more significant things.
- Each day spends at least 30 minutes for self-inquiry because it is essential. If you make it a practice, you will be able to remove codependency from the root. Also, now you know a few factors that might have triggered codependency. Hence, you can engage in meditation or other spiritual activities to handle codependency.
- There can be a lot of things that you love to do apart from taking care of your partner. Maybe you've had hobbies that you gave up, so try to recall them.
- Learn to let others handle their problems all alone without finding solutions for them.
- Know that it is okay to have other feelings aside from happiness, so let others experience negative emotions without rescuing them from it.
- Chant the mantra that you and your preference are essential.
- Be kind even if the world is not. But this doesn't mean you should be hard on yourself while being kind to others.

I know, it is not easy to practice all these tips. But a small change counts so begin small even if seems hard. Also, you don't have to feel awkward about getting professional help because this is about your life and health, so don't think about people's opinions.

Connection with the Childhood

Yes, you already know that codependency has a direct connection with childhood. But let me elaborate it for you. First of all, you must understand the characteristics of a dysfunctional family, so here are the most common ones:
- Unsupportive
- Unsafe and dangerous
- Unpredictable
- Chaotic
- Manipulative
- Physically and emotionally neglectful
- Unnecessary blaming
- Abusive
- Shaming
- Judgmental
- Secretive
- Inattentive
- Denies outside help
- Doesn't accept their mistakes
- Unrealistic expectations

More often, children are blamed for everything, or they are made to believe that there aren't any problems. However, when children are not directed in the right path, they tend to get confused, and they end up assuming that they are the problem. It leads to many negative feelings such as feeling incapable, stupid, unworthy, and much more because of the behaviors of the adults. This settles in the minds of the children and reciprocates when they engage in inmate relationships when they are adults. If your parents were not able to offer a nurturing environment, there could be several drawbacks such as:
- You tend to treat yourself as a people-pleaser. To feel that you have complete control, you start pleasing people around you. Giving becomes a regular thing, and you don't disagree with anything other people say. Only through pleasing people, you nurture your self-worth.
- You put on your parents' shoes, yes, you become the parent. Caretaking becomes a common thing, and a parenting role might not be foreign to you. Since your parents are careless and addicts, you have to make sure that your siblings are taken care of.
- You don't mind getting hurt because it keeps happening. In your

childhood, you have been hurt by your family, both physically and mentally. You've been lied to, threatened, and taken for granted. The same pain keeps coming back through lovers, friends, and everyone you associate closely in adulthood as well. The main reason is that you don't mind getting hurt and you don't speak up!

- You often feel guilty even though you are not at fault. You will easily find a lot of reasons to feel guilty. You worry about not being able to fix your family problems and correct your parents. Many problems can't be fixed or solved, so feeling guilty for such problems is not logical. Yet, as a codependent person, you feel obliged to make corrections and so you often guilty.
- You don't understand how to keep a distance. Keeping boundaries doesn't make sense to you because you are confused. Either you are weak regarding keeping boundaries or too firm. Some codependents are overly pleasing, so they are to be considered as weak, but some codependents are too firm, and they struggle to trust others.
- You are not ready to trust others, not only because of the above reasons but also because you have been betrayed. When you often face betrayals, it is obvious that you will not be ready to trust someone once again. Even though the barrier is praiseworthy, it will keep you away from intimacy with your partner.
- You usually feel alone. You might have had a lot of secrets in your childhood that you did not want to share with anyone. You would have been wondering whether you were the only without a happy family. The loneliness that you have been feeling wouldn't have been pleasant, which is why you remain in an unhealthy relationship. You would rather be with someone than be alone. You assume that loneliness proves that you are unwanted.
- You feel unwanted and imperfect. Remember, nobody is perfect, everyone has their share of mistakes, so if you have flaws, it is okay; you are a human. But it is something that you can't remove from your mind because it has been fed from your childhood. You've been forced to believe that you are flawed. Even if the reality is crystal clear, your mind struggles to differentiate the truth.
- You don't like to seek help. You were the one to help, so it is weird to seek help. You have never been taken care of, so when it happens all of a sudden, it might bother you a little bit. You like to help others than to seek help because you feel comfortable when you are not needy.
- You control others. When there are problems and difficult situations, you try to handle them by ignoring the fact that you are helpless too. You just want to control others and the situation because you have been doing it in your childhood somehow.

- You become the most responsible person. You've been taking care of your family even though you were a child. You've been handling all the responsibilities of an adult. You become the person that anybody can depend on despite the difficulties that you are going through. In fact, you are ready to work overtime to meet the responsibilities. Above all, you assume that you are responsible for the actions and feelings of others.

I know, you can relate to this because any codependent would have been through all these situations. You might even recall some memories from your childhood. Unfortunately, your childhood will have a direct impact on your adulthood. You repeat your behaviors even though they are dangerous and unsatisfying because you have been used from your childhood.

You definitely deserve a healthy relationship, don't let others convince you otherwise. Of course, there are a lot of steps to be taken to overcome codependency, but nothing is impossible. Just think, as a child you can't walk out of your home and live alone because it is impossible. Your codependent behaviors kept you alive as a child, even though the behaviors have to be treated to live a happy adult life. Now you know where the problem started, and you have a clear picture of it. As an adult, you can seek help to overcome the codependency traits, and you can seek happiness!

Repeating the Past: Repetitive Compulsion

Finally, one of the essential factors that you must know about is repeating the past: repetitive compulsion.

"We repeat what we do not repair." —Christine Langley Obaugh

If you analyze the above statement, you will understand how relatable it is! Codependents don't repair, and rather they repeat, which is why they struggle to lead a happy life. In general, why do we repeat the past? Why can't we repair it? If you think about the repetition compulsion, it is about how a person repeats the traumatic circumstances. This means you are pulling yourself into a situation that might happen again, just like in the past. For some people walking out of a relationship seem harsh because of repetitive compulsion. Most traumatized individuals willingly expose themselves to events and situations that reenact the traumas. But they will not be conscious of their behavior in the early stages of their life.

But why do you think it is so hard to change? Generally, humans feel comfortable doing the things that are predictable and known. Of course, sometimes such things might be harmful to their emotional and physical well-being, yet they go for it. For example, many people remain or return to an abusive relationship, even though it is not healthy for them. However, there are some valid reasons why you repeat your past so here are some examples:

- Reenacting history while assuming that you could control things that you weren't able to do as a child.
- You repeat the past with the hope of seeing a change, meaning you believe that you will be able to get it right. You start to change yourself in a way to be liked by your partner and believe that you satisfy him or her.
- You behave as if you deserve being mistreated.
- Compulsive repetition may offer short-term pleasure and a sense of pride, but in the long run, it progresses to negative behaviors and emotions.

Yes, the change will not be easy, but it is essential for your health and life. You might like the predictable lifestyle, but ultimately, you will end up trapped in the path of codependency. You must move out of it to enjoy the real beauty of life.

Before you react like in the past, think whether you want to be stuck in the place you were years ago or you want to move on and enjoy life. Your style of repeating the trauma will be analyzed and understood by the therapist if you are looking for professional help. But if you are not ready for professional help, you must make sure to learn and understand your style of repeating trauma through self-assessment.

In fact, all the above factors are interrelated if you analyze them deeply. The repetitive compulsion is directly related to childhood experiences. It is much better to seek professional help. Meanwhile, you have to build a healthy relationship with your mind. If you are in a calm state, you will be able to think straight, which will help you in decision making and overcoming unhealthy behaviors.

4 FACTORS THAT SUSTAIN CODEPENDENCY: THE SNOWBALL EFFECT

Often codependency continues to perpetuate due to different reasons. As a codependent person, you must make an effort to understand the reasons that sustain codependency so that you can look for ways to overcome those. You are your own enemy and which is why you struggle to overcome codependency. Sabotaging yourself becomes a constant thing assuming that you don't deserve a good life. Of course, you might have made some mistakes in your past, who doesn't? But not forgiving yourself for past mistakes is not the right decision. You start denying your own strengths and thoughts. There are different ways of self-sabotage, including codependency, aggression, an abusive relationship, denial, and more.

Even after realizing codependency, you will not be able to overcome it because of self-sabotage which can make you feel unworthy which triggers codependency even deeper. To treat codependency, you must believe that you are worthy. You should think of the way a person with self-love would handle the situation that you are in. A person with self-love will not select unhealthy options that might hurt their mind and body.

If you can't love yourself yet, try to fake it for some time and so you will gradually make it true. Self-sabotaging is closing the actual view, which is why you are struggling to see the reality, so when you fake it, you will be able to clear the path slowly, but firmly. If you consider factors like anger, denial, and shame, they perpetuate codependency pretty easily. Hence, you must educate yourself about the factors so you can overcome them.

Anger and denial regarding codependency and your partner

Codependency should not be denied because it is dangerous. If you are denying it, it means you are not ready to accept and change, hence it will continue to remain. Instead of facing the problems in your life, you try harder to save others from facing their problems. The same behavior repeats itself when you deny the fact that you are codependent. Basically, there are different types of denial that you will learn below. Once you understand the types, you can take necessary measures. Even if it's hard to find solutions all alone, it is okay because I'll be discussing the solutions to overcome dependency in the following chapters.

Denial of Your Partner's Behavior

Denying your partner's behavior is one of the common denials, but you can overcome it. You deny that your partner is addicted and his or her addiction causes a lot of problems in your life. Yet, you are not ready to accept it, which is why codependency perpetuates in your life. This kind of denial is common because codependents have been facing similar situations from their childhood. They might have grown up with parents who are addicts, so it looks normal to them.

The addicts and dependents have gotten used to been taken care of, so they are not ready to take responsibility. And codependents are okay with that because they like to take care of others.

If you deny your partner's behaviors, you must understand that you are walking towards a dangerous destination. You must acknowledge the reality and work accordingly because a relationship can ruin your life if you don't handle it wisely. You must accept the fact that you are not responsible for their behaviors. If they are addicted or relying on you for almost everything, it means you have created the path for it. You should not let anyone hurt you just because you are codependent. Also, if you deny your partner's behaviors, it doesn't mean that you don't care about them. Of course, you are bothered, but you just don't see the seriousness, or you somehow build up reasons to justify the act. This is the typical behavior of someone who loves their partner, but the love codependents show is extra. They don't make an effort to correct the mistakes; they just ignore them. However ignorance will make things worse.

Denial of Codependency

When you are confronted about codependency, you will deny it, and that's the very first step. You can clearly see that you are codependent, but you are not ready to accept it because you think it's a situation that has made you a codependent. You try to blame the situation and people so that you don't have to discuss codependency. Most codependents don't want to discuss it because they think it will worsen the pain, but it will not. This is one of the reasons why you deny that you are codependent.

Another reason is you are not someone who seeks help from others so if you accept that you are a codependent you'd have to get help from others to treat it. This kind of mentality leads you towards a destructive path. You don't like the fact that someone is taking care of you and being responsible for your behaviors because, for a long time, you've been doing it for others. You don't want others to make you happy as it triggers self-examination at a point. When you are codependent, you can easily avoid self-examination, which is why you turned down help from others.

Denying your true nature, which is codependency, will help you to stay away from professional help and admitting your codependent nature. On the other hand, some codependents don't seek professional help, but they try to treat themselves all alone. They believe that they can figure out the problem by talking to close friends and reading reliable books and articles. But sometimes, this can be dangerous depending on the level of codependency that you have. You may be ashamed to seek help, so you try not to get in touch with professionals. But remember, it is not a wise move.

Denial of Feelings

This is another type of denial which deals with a codependent's feelings. You are not ready to discuss how you feel, and ultimately, you end up denying your feelings. Normally, codependents can easily understand what other people feel and worry about. Plus, codependents spend a lot of time helping others to feel better. But they deny their own feelings which create resentment in their hearts. Codependency gives rise to obsession. When you are obsessed, you get distracted from what's important. Similarly, when you are obsessed with your partner, it will be hard to focus on your feelings because you are worried about your partner's feelings more than yours. If you think about your own feelings and how you have been doing, you will have no solid answers because you have denied your feelings.

Even if you understand your physical pain, you will not understand emotional pain because you are blinded by codependency. Also, growing up, you have not had an environment that lets you share your emotions and feelings. You may have always been the one to listen, not the one to speak.

Moreover, you don't understand the reason why you should share your feelings when nobody is there to comfort or listen. Hence you keep denying your feelings from childhood. Actually, feelings serve a purpose even if they are not positive feelings. Through feelings, you understand what you need and don't. If you want to interact with people, you must have the ability to share your feelings. How do feelings help you become better at interacting while overcoming codependency?

- If you are angry, you will be reacting to make changes.
- If you are sad, you will empathize and value human connections.
- If you fear, you will keep dangers at bay even if they are emotional dangers.
- If you are guilty, you will have values that you respect.
- If you feel ashamed, you will not harm others.
- If you feel lonely, you will strengthen your connection with others.

Likewise, every negative feeling serves a purpose. When you deny your own feelings, you won't be able to move forward in life. You will bottle up your feelings for years, and it will always be there in your subconscious mind. When you accumulate pain, you will not be able to overcome it. Instead, constant denial might be your answer. What will happen when you continue to deny your feelings? You will end up depressed, and depression isn't as easy as you think!

Maybe you don't, but most codependents treat resentment as a shield to hide anger. Of course, your past or childhood would have been unpleasant and difficult. Maybe you couldn't express what you feel because nobody bothered to listen but that doesn't mean it will repeat in the future unless you want it to repeat. If you stop denying your feelings, you will be able to lead a healthy and happy life. It is important to talk to your partner and explain how you feel because unlike other healthy relationships, your partner will not understand your feelings. Not because he or she doesn't understand others, but because you have been hiding your feelings from them.

Unresolved feelings will repeat itself. If you overcome denial and anger, you will be able to overcome codependency too. But if you don't, it will perpetuate. And you must learn about the snowball effect to understand sustaining codependency.

The Snowball Effect

This is a concept discussed in psychology to understand something that is not only related to codependency but also many other things in life. We all have dealt with the snowball effect in life. Many times in life, you would have dealt with situations that you thought wouldn't blow up this big, but before you know it, the situation becomes a huge mess. This is metaphorical to a snowball that rolls down the hill and forms something huge. Just like that, the negative feelings and thoughts about yourself can snowball into something huge, and before you know it, there would have been a huge mess. You will not be able to cope with yourself when the snowball gets smashed and creates a huge mess! Certain thoughts make the whole process of opening up to your partner difficult, and some of them are:

- You tend to jump into conclusions without focusing on the evidence.
- You tend to generalize even if you see a single negative thing to support certain activity.
- You often catastrophize because you only think about the worst possible outcome.
- You easily filter the positive things into negative.
- You set strict rules regarding the unrealistic expectation of yours and others.

These negative feelings will increase your anxiety and enhance your negative mindset. When your mind is filtered through these feelings, it can be complicated to see things in the right way. You will not make an effort to change or to motivate yourself to overcome codependency because your mind is filtered that way. If negative emotions and behaviors snowball down the hill, you will not be able to stop it successfully. Hence, you must stop it when it started. Well, stopping the snowball where it started might impossible, but it is not. If you follow a few essential points, you will be able to do it.

- The critical point is to break the chain. Start by challenging a few thoughts and looking at them objectively.
- Write your feelings down or talk to a close friend about it. Also, when talking to them about your feelings if they have something to say, let them because listening is also essential.
- Don't skip your day-to-day activities because when you have a routine, you will be able to distract negative thinking for some time.
- Do engage in mindful activities, exercises, and yoga.

These tips might look simple, but they are not as easy as they sound because consistency and patience are two essential things when you are trying to overcome codependency. If you try to move out of this vicious cycle in one go, you are likely to get hurt. Instead, baby steps will help you overcome codependency without creating a mess. Don't let your mind snowball in the process of healing, so even the process of healing should be done step by step.

Not to forget that a professional can help you out of this vicious circle simply because he or she has the skills and required education. Hence, don't step back if you need professional help.

5 WAYS TO RECOVER FROM A CODEPENDENT RELATIONSHIP

Now that you have a clear picture of codependency, you can explore ways to overcome it. It is possible to overcome codependency if you know a few ways to recover from it. It might take some time to heal because it has been rooted in your mind, and you have been hurt beyond limits. But if you are consistent and dedicated towards the change, you will be able to achieve it.

Understanding Your Relationship In-Depth

Change begins from you. If you want to change, you must accept that you are codependent. Accepting it is the biggest step towards the change. Before you clear the path, you must analyze your role in this relationship. Maybe you control your partner, or maybe you don't let them take responsibility for their mistakes. Maybe they're constantly on your mind and you speak about them too often. You must think about whether you bring them in whenever you are speaking to someone else. Or perhaps you are a compulsive caregiver. Your codependent behavior begins when you start caring for your partner while sacrificing your own health. Of course, you can take care of your partner, and it is essential, but not at the cost of your own health. When you are in a relationship, both you and your partner's health matter.

Another important thing that you must carefully analyze is whether you forgive your partner for obvious mistakes too easily. You are ready to forgive your partner because you believe that if you don't, he or she might leave you and you don't like being alone. However, when this habit continues, you will end up feeling responsible for your partner's wrong choices, and it is not healthy for you.

Ultimately, if you feel that you are not satisfied with this relationship, yet you are forcing yourself to remain because you like to be with someone who makes you feel valued. This is the stage where you should realize that serious help is needed because this is an addiction.

When you realize that you are addicted to the relationship, you should pat yourself on the back because you've understood your role. It is time to think about what you really wanted from this relationship: why did you start this relationship in the first place? What was the reason? When you build confidence, you will be able to find your way out of codependency.

Overcoming the Addiction

The next most significant step is to overcome the addiction. There are different ways to overcome addiction, but begin by stepping out of the comfort zone. I know it's easier said than done, but trust me, I have seen many individuals succeeding in life after coming out of their protective shells. If you hide, you will not reach the potential or find better opportunities. Similarly, if you don't step out, you will not realize what the world has for you. When you center your life around one person, your view is limited to that person. Hence you don't get the chance to grow.

To step out of comfort zone, break the habit and remove yourself from the person you have been attached to. This doesn't mean you should break up. You must start exploring new things, new friendships, activities, and exciting things. When you start collecting new experiences, you will realize that you have been behind closed doors for so long, and you will regret it.

Once you step out, you will have a broader mindset, so start questioning why you do this to yourself. What do you get by being codependent? Why don't you spend time to realize the importance of independence? What have you achieved so far by being codependent? This self-assessment will help you when you are trying to remove yourself from codependency.

After the self-assessment, you can think about your needs and their value. What are the needs? Why do people give so much importance to needs? And what are your needs? Are your needs essential too? If yes, why are they important? Don't try to answer all these questions in one go. Instead, take time and think and analyze. First, you must value yourself to understand the value of the needs you have.

Typically, codependents are fed the thoughts that their needs are less important when compared to others' needs. Understanding the wrong reason is essential to understand your needs. You must realize that your body and health are also significant and need special care just like you care for your partner. One of the best ways to overcome codependency is to recognize the importance of your needs and health. Once you identify your needs, you will have to get the awareness that is required. And then, focus on prioritizing your needs above others so that you get the happiness that was missing in your life.

Building up the Courage to Say 'Goodbye.'

Mustering up the courage to say goodbye is another essential step of removing codependency. As a codependent, it is not going to be easy for you because even an independent person struggles to say 'goodbye'. But what's important is the courage that you build up and preparing yourself to do it. Above all, be proud of yourself for getting ready to face this without letting codependency eat you.

Yes, the initial stage of your relationship would have been fun and complete, but down the road, you will realize the real taste. The bitter truth behind the codependent relationship is the romantic love injected by the world. It is assumed that love is strong and pure only when two people are romantically involved, but it is not the case. Most codependents believe sticking with their partner 24/7 is what makes a relationship true. Well, it is not true, you must get the chance to grow and develop when you are in a relationship. If you and your partner's growth is held back, it is time to give up on the relationship and focus on your codependent nature.

Most codependents think sharing the life itself is what a relationship stands for, but it is not; sharing life experiences is what relationship stands for. If you are losing yourself in your partner, you need serious help, and the help is walking out of the relationship and working on yourself. If you want to work on yourself, it is important to wave 'goodbye' to your relationship even if it is hard. You should continue your journey to find yourself.

To successfully find yourself, you must remain single for some time and get along with yourself. You must understand who you are and what you want.

Taking the Time to Lament

You are not a robot, so you will be worried and depressed and moreover, you won't like being alone. Breaking up with your partner is crucial to find yourself and to become a better person. It will hurt you as you are in a state of confusion, depression, and pain. You might feel as if the world is collapsing but hang in there. You will reach your goal soon. Think about why you started this journey of finding yourself. What will you get by finding out who you are? Why can't you be codependent? Why aren't codependent relationships encouraged? And why do you yearn for the enjoyment in an interdependent relationship? Likewise, you must think of all these things while lamenting.

Of course, lamenting will make you feel better, but sometimes it might take you back to where you were, hence rethinking these questions will keep you on the track. When you are lamenting, think why you ended this relationship. Think about the benefit both you and your partner will receive. Don't remain inside your home. Go out and do something even if you don't feel like doing it. Be confident and happy about your decision because it is the right decision even if you are feeling terrible about it. Of course, don't hold back tears; cry, and let it wash away your pain. Crying is not a shame; you have all the liberty to cry, so do it! You will be able to overcome this stage by following the tips I have mentioned.

Creating a Newer Version of Yourself

The most important step of all is to create a newer version of yourself. Do you really think it is going to be easy? No, but is it going to be worthy and you will be excited to explore and enjoy yourself. In the path of creating a newer version of yourself, think about building an interdependent relationship once you move out from codependency, it will boost more energy to the process. Examine and correct your own behaviors. You have been looking down upon yourself since long, but in this process, you must think about the good things and the best details about yourself. Start focusing on your beliefs and values, and learn to respect them. Above all, accept the fact you are not liable to anyone. You don't have to prove your worth to someone else.

You might have a lot of self-judgments, think about them and correct. Most judgments might be uncompassionate and rude, so try to see good things about yourself and be kind. If you are not kind to yourself, how can you be kind to your partner? Being kind requires nothing, so why not? Keep reminding yourself that seeking help is not shameful or unhealthy, so you should ask for help and grow. You should help others while letting them help you. Seeking help is actually a strength that you must build up. Lower your shield of fear and let people come into yourself. Connect with them honestly and be ready to share your opinions and views even if they don't accept it. Don't fear rejection because rejection helps you grow. Grow into a better version of yourself because you are capable of it!

Collecting Unique Experiences and Rebuilding Your Reliance

This is an exciting step, so try to get the best out of it. You will be discovering a lot of unique things so you will be exposed to better opportunities. To rebuild your reliance, you must focus on a few crucial things. Before you keep the step to trust another individual, you must complete the path of understanding who you are!

You must start by writing a gratitude journal, and if you don't like writing a journal, write about something that you feel blessed about every day. Also, something interesting that you can do is to create a list with 25 things that you love about yourself. Don't underestimate the power of this tip because it is not easy. When you are writing the things that you love about yourself, you can add the things that you are looking to improve. When you dig deeper, you will start to realize yourself even better, and it is going to be awesome.

Don't overlook meditation even if you don't feel like doing it, and you must allocate some time for meditation. If you want to recover from codependency soon, the best option is to spend time meditating. When you meditate, you'll hear your inner voice louder, and you'll be focused so that you understand what it says. You will be calm throughout the session, and it will reduce stress as well. Through meditation, you'll understand a lot of great things because it is time you spend with yourself all alone.

So now, when rebuilding your reliance, you have to be careful, but steady. When selecting someone new, make sure that they have high self-esteem and are not codependent. Remember, you should not be in a hurry to start another relationship because the time alone will help you make the right decision.

Learning to Live While Prioritizing Self-Care

Lastly, don't ever give up on self-care. As a codependent person, you wouldn't have thought about self-care, but now, you are becoming a newer version of yourself. You are developing self-love so don't overlook self-care. Make it your priority and learn to live while giving the best to yourself and others!

To prioritize self-care, you must understand the beauty of saying 'no,' and making it crystal clear. Exercising isn't just to stay fit, and it is an overall thing that keeps your body and your mind healthy. It is one of the most important steps of self-care. Have your 'alone time' because it is essential to pamper yourself by watching your favorite TV show, reading a book that you love, or even taking a long shower. Don't forget to connect with people as it keeps you on the go.

Although there are many other tips to enhance self-care, the ones I've listed will help you to shape yourself into a better person.

You are the ONLY light in your darkest days of lives, hence appreciate it!.

CONCLUSION

Now that you've concluded The Codependency Help Book: How to Fix a Codependent Relationship Book, you are ready to identify codependency—and more importantly overcome captivating nature or traits.

You understand that it takes time to find out whether you are in a codependent relationship or not. Most people don't want to accept the fact that they are in a codependent relationship, so they pretend to be "happy." As mentioned in the book, if you fake it, you will not make it till the end. There will be a lot of psychological issues that you might have to deal with if you pretend to be "happy." Instead, you can focus on fixing the problems or moving out of the relationship.

There's nothing you can do by continuing a codependent relationship without fixing it. The more you tolerate, the further you fall, so do you want to fall or fight back? It can be tough in the beginning when you realize that you are in a codependent relationship, and you see all the signs mentioned in the book in your relationship. But it is never too late to correct and move forward. After all, humans are flawed, and remember, being an imperfect human is not a mistake. You can amend your mistakes through proper guidance, and this book is the guidance required to fix your codependent relationship.

Made in the USA
Columbia, SC
06 November 2019